To

_____

From

_____

Date

_____

Worship

INSPIRATION FOR EVERYDAY LIFE

MAX LUCADO

THOMAS NELSON
Since 1798

Published in Nashville, Tennessee, by Thomas Nelson. Thomas Nelson is a registered trademark of HarperCollins Christian Publishing, Inc.

Thomas Nelson titles may be purchased in bulk for educational, business, fund-raising, or sales promotional use. For information, please e-mail SpecialMarkets@ThomasNelson.com.

Scripture quotations marked ESV are from the ESV® Bible (The Holy Bible, English Standard Version®). Copyright © 2001 by Crossway, a publishing ministry of Good News Publishers. Used by permission. All rights reserved.

Scripture quotations marked THE MESSAGE are from *The Message*. Copyright © by Eugene H. Peterson 1993, 1994, 1995, 1996, 2000, 2001, 2002. Used by permission of Tyndale House Publishers, Inc.

Scripture quotations marked NASB are from New American Standard Bible®. Copyright © 1960, 1962, 1963, 1968, 1971, 1972, 1973, 1975, 1977, 1995 by The Lockman Foundation. Used by permission. (www.Lockman.org)

Scripture quotations marked NCV are from the New Century Version®. © 2005 by Thomas Nelson. Used by permission. All rights reserved.

Scripture quotations marked NIV are from the Holy Bible, New International Version®, NIV®. Copyright © 1973, 1978, 1984, 2011 by Biblica, Inc.® Used by permission of Zondervan. All rights reserved worldwide. www.zondervan.com. The "NIV" and "New International Version" are trademarks registered in the United States Patent and Trademark Office by Biblica, Inc.®

Scripture quotations marked NLT are from the *Holy Bible*, New Living Translation. © 1996, 2004, 2007, 2013 by Tyndale House Foundation. Used by permission of Tyndale House Publishers, Inc., Carol Stream, Illinois 60188. All rights reserved.

Scripture quotations marked TLB are from The Living Bible. Copyright © 1971. Used by permission of Tyndale House Publishers, Inc., Carol Stream, Illinois 60188. All rights reserved.

Any Internet addresses, phone numbers, or company or product information printed in this book are offered as a resource and are not intended in any way to be or to imply an endorsement by Thomas Nelson, nor does Thomas Nelson vouch for the existence, content, or services of these sites, phone numbers, companies, or products beyond the life of this book.

Library of Congress Cataloging-in-Publication Data

ISBN 978-0-7180-9137-8

Printed in China

17 18 19 20 21 RRD 10 9 8 7 6 5 4 3 2 1

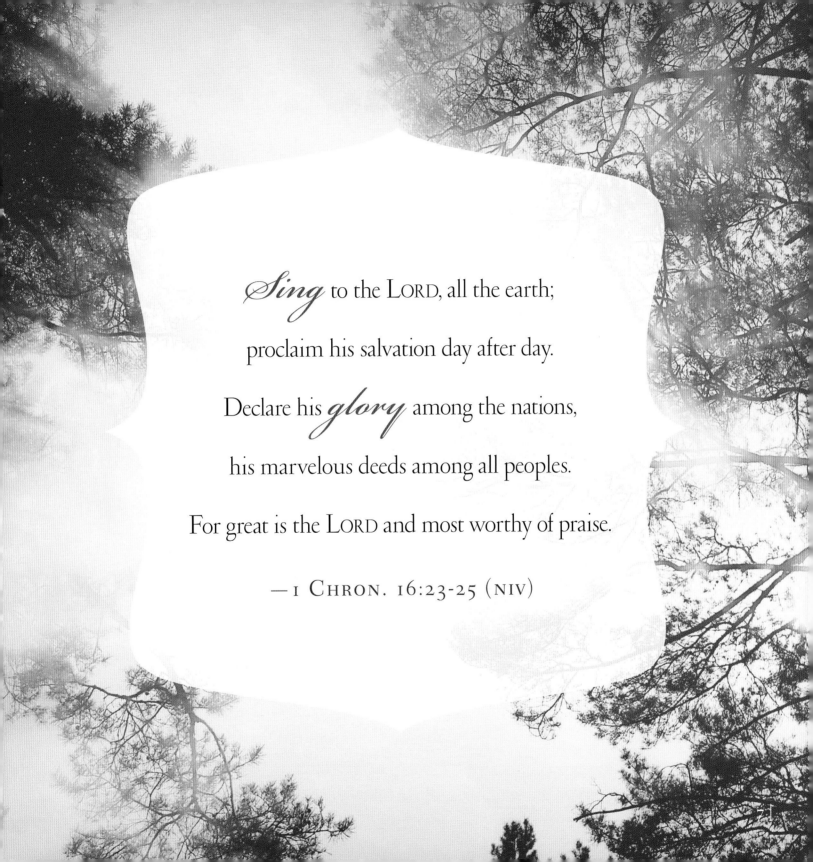

Sing to the LORD, all the earth;

proclaim his salvation day after day.

Declare his *glory* among the nations,

his marvelous deeds among all peoples.

For great is the LORD and most worthy of praise.

— I CHRON. 16:23-25 (NIV)

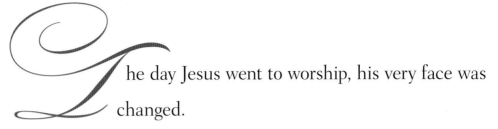

he day Jesus went to worship, his very face was changed.

"You're telling me that Jesus went to worship?"

I am. The Bible speaks of a day when Jesus took time to stand with friends in the presence of God. Let's read about the day Jesus went to worship:

> Six days later, Jesus took Peter, James, and John, the brother of James, up on a high mountain by themselves. While they watched, Jesus' appearance was changed; his face became bright like the sun, and his clothes became white as light. Then Moses and Elijah appeared to them, talking with Jesus.
>
> Peter said to Jesus, "Lord, it is good that we are here. If you want, I will put up three tents here—one for you, one for Moses, and one for Elijah."

While Peter was talking, a bright cloud covered them. A voice came from the cloud and said, "This is my Son, whom I love, and I am very pleased with him. Listen to him!" (Matt. 17:1–5 NCV)

The words of Matthew presuppose a decision on the part of Jesus to stand in the presence of God. The simple fact that he chose his companions and went up on a mountain suggests this was no spur-of-the-moment action. He didn't awaken one morning, look at the calendar and then at his watch, and say, "Oops, today is the day we go to the mountain." No, he had preparations to make. Ministry to people was suspended so ministry to his heart could occur. Since his chosen place of worship was some distance away, he had to select the right path and stay on the right road. By the time he was on the mountain, his heart was ready. Jesus prepared for worship.

Let me ask you, do you do the same? Do you prepare for worship? What paths do you take to lead you up the mountain? The question may

seem foreign, but my hunch is, many of us simply wake up and show up. We're sadly casual when it comes to meeting God.

Would we be so lackadaisical with, oh, let's say, the president? Suppose you were granted a Sunday morning breakfast at the White House? How would you spend Saturday night? Would you get ready? Would you collect your thoughts? Would you think about your questions and requests? Of course you would. Should we prepare any less for an encounter with the Holy God?

Let me urge you to come to worship prepared to worship. Pray before you come so you will be ready to pray when you arrive. Sleep before you come so you'll stay alert when you arrive. Read the Word before you come so your heart will be soft when you worship. Come hungry. Come willing. Come expecting God to speak.

—Just Like Jesus

Most people suffer from small thoughts about God. In an effort to see him as our friend, we have lost his immensity. In our desire to understand him, we have sought to contain him. The God of the Bible cannot be contained. He brought order out of chaos and created creation. With a word he called Adam out of dust and Eve out of a bone. He consulted no committee. He sought no counsel.

He has no peer.

—BEFORE AMEN

Great is the

LORD in Zion;

he is *exalted* over

all the nations.

—PSALM 99:2 (NIV)

The chief reason for *applauding* God?

He *deserves* it.

We worship God because we need to. But our need runs a turtle-paced distant second to the thoroughbred reason for worship.

The chief reason for applauding God? He deserves it. If singing did nothing but weary your voice, if giving only emptied your wallet—if worship did nothing for you—it would still be right to do. God warrants our worship.

How else do you respond to a Being of blazing, blistering, unadulterated, unending holiness? No mark. Nor freckle. Not a bad thought, bad day, or bad decision. Ever! What do you do with such holiness if not adore it?

And his power. He churns forces that launch meteors, orbit planets, and ignite stars. Commanding whales to spout salty air, petunias to perfume the night, and songbirds to chirp joy into spring. Above the earth, flotillas of clouds endlessly shape and reshape; within the earth, strata of groaning rocks shift and turn. Who are we to sojourn on a trembling, wonderful orb so shot through with wonder?

And tenderness? God has never taken his eyes off you. Not for a millisecond. He's always near. He lives to hear your heartbeat. He loves to hear your prayers. He'd die for your sin before he'd let you die in your sin, so he did.

What do you do with such a Savior? Don't you sing to him? Don't you celebrate him in baptism, elevate him in Communion? Don't you bow a knee, lower a head, hammer a nail, feed the poor, and lift up your gift in worship? Of course you do.

Worship God. Applaud him loud and often. For your sake, you need it.

And for heaven's sake, he deserves it.

—CURE FOR THE COMMON LIFE

O *magnify* the

LORD with me,

and let us *exalt*

His name together.

—PSALM 34:3 (NASB)

The purpose of worship is to change
the face of the worshiper.

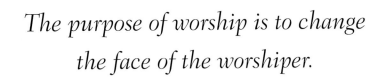

This is exactly what happened to Christ on the mountain. Jesus' appearance was changed: "His face became bright like the sun" (Matt. 17:2 NCV).

The connection between the face and worship is more than coincidental. Our face is the most public part of our bodies, covered less than any other area. It is also the most recognizable part of our bodies. We don't fill a school annual with photos of people's feet but rather with photos of faces. God desires to take our faces, this exposed and memorable part of our bodies, and use them to reflect his goodness. Paul writes: "Our faces, then, are not covered. We all show the Lord's glory, and we are being changed to be like him. This change in us brings ever greater glory, which comes from the Lord, who is the Spirit" (2 Cor. 3:18 NCV).

God invites us to see his face so he can change ours. He uses our uncovered faces to display his glory. The transformation isn't easy. The sculptor of Mount Rushmore faced a lesser challenge than does God. But our Lord is up to the task. He loves to change the faces of his children. By his fingers, wrinkles of worry are rubbed away. Shadows of shame and doubt become portraits of grace and trust. He relaxes clenched jaws and smooths furrowed brows. His touch can remove the bags of exhaustion from beneath the eyes and turn tears of despair into tears of peace.

How? Through worship.

We'd expect something more complicated, more demanding. A forty-day fast or the memorization of Leviticus perhaps. No. God's plan is simpler. He changes our faces through worship.

Exactly what is worship? I like King David's definition. "O magnify

the LORD with me, and let us exalt His name together" (Ps. 34:3 NASB). Worship is the act of magnifying God. Enlarging our vision of him. Stepping into the cockpit to see where he sits and observe how he works. Of course, his size doesn't change, but our perception of him does. As we draw nearer, he seems larger. Isn't that what we need? A *big* view of God? Don't we have *big* problems, *big* worries, *big* questions? Of course we do. Hence we need a big view of God.

Worship offers that. How can we sing, "Holy, Holy, Holy" and not have our vision expanded? Or what about the lines from Horatio G. Spafford in "It Is Well with My Soul"?

> *My sin—O the bliss of this glorious thought,*
> *My sin—not in part but the whole,*
> *Is nailed to the cross and I bear it no more,*
> *Praise the Lord, praise the Lord, O my soul!*

Can we sing those words and not have our countenance illuminated?

A vibrant, shining face is the mark of one who has stood in God's presence. After speaking to God, Moses had to cover his face with a veil (Exod. 34:33–35). After seeing heaven, Stephen's face glowed like that of an angel (Acts 6:15; 7:55–56). God is in the business of changing the face of the world.

Let me be very clear. This change is his job, not ours. Our goal is not to make our faces radiant. Not even Jesus did that. Matthew says, "Jesus' appearance was changed" not "Jesus changed his appearance."

Moses didn't even know his face was shining (Exod. 34:29). Our goal is not to conjure up some fake, frozen expression. Our goal is simply to stand before God with a prepared and willing heart and then let God do his work.

And he does. He wipes away the tears. He mops away the perspiration. He softens our furrowed brows. He touches our cheeks. He changes our faces as we worship.

—JUST LIKE JESUS

God does not exist to make a big *deal* out of us. We *exist* to make a big deal out of him. It's *not* about you. It's not about me. It's all about *him.*

—It's Not About Me

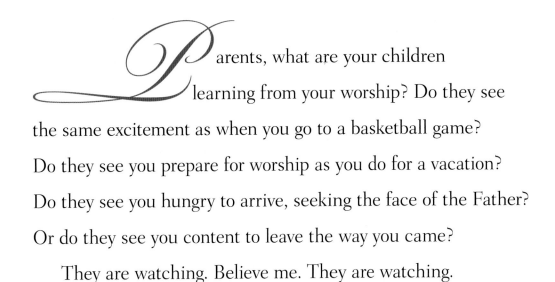

arents, what are your children learning from your worship? Do they see the same excitement as when you go to a basketball game? Do they see you prepare for worship as you do for a vacation? Do they see you hungry to arrive, seeking the face of the Father? Or do they see you content to leave the way you came?

They are watching. Believe me. They are watching.

Do you come to church with a worship-hungry heart? Our Savior did.

May I urge you to be just like Jesus? Prepare your heart for worship. Let God change your face through worship. Demonstrate the power of worship.

—JUST LIKE JESUS

Listening to God is a firsthand experience. When he asks for your *attention,* God doesn't want you to send a substitute; he wants you. He invites you to vacation in his splendor. He *invites* you to feel the touch of his hand. He invites you to *feast* at his table. He wants to spend time with you. And with a little training, your time with God can be the *highlight* of your day.

—JUST LIKE JESUS

Forget greatness; seek *littleness*. Trust more; strut less. Make lots of requests, and *accept* all the gifts. Come to God the way a *child* comes to Daddy.

—BEFORE AMEN

Jesus Christ is the same *yesterday* and *today* and *forever.*

—Hebrews 13:8 (esv)

God will always be the same.

No one else will. Lovers call you today and scorn you tomorrow. Companies follow pay raises with pink slips. Friends applaud you when you drive a classic and dismiss you when you drive a dud. Not God. God is "always the same" (Ps. 102:27 NLT).

With him "there is no variation or shadow due to change" (James 1:17 ESV).

Catch God in a bad mood? Won't happen. Fear exhausting his grace? A sardine will swallow the Atlantic first. Think he's given up on you? Wrong. Did he not make a promise to you? "God is not a human being, and he will not lie. He is not a human, and he does not change his mind. What he says he will do, he does. What he promises, he makes come true" (Num. 23:19 NCV). He's never sullen or sour, sulking or stressed. His strength, truth, ways, and love never change. He is "the same yesterday and today and forever" (Heb. 13:8 ESV).

—It's Not About Me

God
rewards
those
who
seek
him.

*G*od rewards those who seek him. Not those who seek doctrine or religion or systems or creeds. Many settle for these lesser passions, but the reward goes to those who settle for nothing less than Jesus himself. And what is the reward? What awaits those who seek Jesus? Nothing short of the heart of Jesus. "And as the Spirit of the Lord works within us, we become more and more like him" (2 Cor. 3:18 TLB).

Can you think of a greater gift than to be like Jesus? Christ felt no guilt; God wants to banish yours. Jesus had no bad habits; God wants to remove yours. Jesus had no fear of death; God wants you to be fearless. Jesus had kindness for the diseased and mercy for the rebellious and courage for the challenges. God wants you to have the same.

—JUST LIKE JESUS

God will *whisper*. He will shout. He will touch and tug. He will take away our *burdens;* he'll even take away our *blessings*. If there are a thousand steps between us and him, he will take all but one. But he will leave the final one for us. The *choice* is ours. Please understand. His goal is not to make you happy. His *goal* is to make you his.

—A GENTLE THUNDER

God in us! Have we sounded the depth of this promise?

God was with Adam and Eve, walking with them in the cool of the evening.

God was *with* Abraham, even calling the patriarch his friend.

God was *with* Moses and the children of Israel. Parents could point their children to the fire by night and cloud by day; *God is with us*, they could assure.

Between the cherubim of the ark, in the glory of the temple, God was *with* his people. He was *with* the apostles. Peter could touch God's beard. John could watch God sleep. Multitudes could hear his voice. God was *with* them!

But he is *in* you. You are a modern-day Mary. Even more

so. He was a fetus in her, but he is a force in you. He will do what you cannot. Imagine a million dollars being deposited into your checking account. To any observer you look the same, except for the goofy smile, but are you? Not at all! With God *in* you, you have a million resources that you did not have before!

Can't stop drinking? Christ can. And he lives within you.

Can't stop worrying? Christ can. And he lives within you.

Can't forgive the jerk, forget the past, or forsake your bad habits? Christ can! And he lives within you.

Paul knew this. "For this purpose also I labor, striving according to His power, which mightily works with*in* me" (Col. 1:29, NASB).

—NEXT DOOR SAVIOR

Like Mary,
you and I are
indwelt
by Christ.

—Next Door Savior

God calls us in a real world. He doesn't communicate by performing tricks. He doesn't communicate by stacking stars in the heavens or reincarnating grandparents from the grave. He's not going to speak to you through voices in a cornfield or a little fat man in a land called Oz. There is about as much power in the plastic Jesus that's on your dashboard as there is in the Styrofoam dice on your rearview mirror.

It doesn't make a lick of difference if you are an Aquarius or a Capricorn or if you were born the day Kennedy was shot. God's not a trickster. He's not a genie. He's not a magician or a good luck charm or the man upstairs. He is, instead, the Creator of the universe who is right here in the thick of our day-to-day world, who speaks to you more through cooing babies and hungry bellies than he ever will through horoscopes, zodiac papers, or weeping Madonnas.

If you get some supernatural vision or hear some strange voice in the night, don't get too carried away. It could be God or it could be indigestion, and you don't want to misinterpret one for the other.

Nor do you want to miss the impossible by looking for the incredible.

God speaks in our world. We just have to learn to hear him.

Listen for him amidst the ordinary.

—AND THE ANGELS WERE SILENT

Listen

for him

amidst the

ordinary.

Ascribe to the LORD, you *heavenly* beings,

ascribe to the LORD glory and *strength*.

Ascribe to the LORD the *glory* due his name;

worship the LORD in the splendor of his holiness.

—PSALM 29:1-2 (NIV)

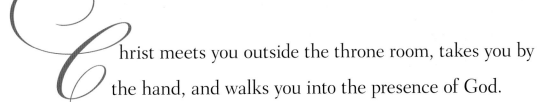

hrist meets you outside the throne room, takes you by the hand, and walks you into the presence of God.

Upon entrance we find grace, not condemnation; mercy, not punishment. Where we would never be granted an audience with the king, we are now welcomed into his presence.

If you are a parent you understand this. If a child you don't know appears on your doorstep and asks to spend the night, what would you do? Likely you would ask him his name, where he lives, find out why he is roaming the streets, and contact his parents. On the other hand, if a youngster enters your house escorted by your child, that child is welcome. The same is true with God. By becoming friends with the Son we gain access to the Father.

By becoming friends with the Son we gain access to the Father.

Jesus promised, "All those who stand before others and say they believe in me, I will say before my Father in heaven that they belong to me" (Matt. 10:32 NCV). Because we are friends of his Son, we have entrance to the throne room. He ushers us into that "blessing of God's grace that we now enjoy" (Rom. 5:2 NCV).

This gift is not an occasional visit before God but rather a permanent "access by faith into this grace in which we now stand" (v. 2 NIV).

—IN THE GRIP OF GRACE

John teaches us that the *strongest* relationship with Christ may not necessarily be a *complicated* one.

73

I like John most for the way he loved Jesus. His relationship with Jesus was, again, rather simple. To John, Jesus was a good friend with a good heart and a good idea. A once-upon-a-time storyteller with a somewhere-over-the-rainbow promise.

One gets the impression that to John, Jesus was above all a loyal companion. Messiah? Yes. Son of God? Indeed. Miracle worker? That, too. But more than anything Jesus was a pal. Someone you could go camping with or bowling with or count the stars with.

Simple. To John, Jesus wasn't a treatise on social activism, nor was he a license for blowing up abortion clinics or living in a desert. Jesus was a friend.

Now what do you do with a friend? (Well, that's rather simple too.) You stick by him.

Maybe that is why John is the only one of the twelve who was at the cross. He came to say good-bye. By his own admission he hadn't quite put the pieces together yet. But that didn't really matter. As far as he was concerned, his closest friend was in trouble and he came to help.

"Can you take care of my mother?"

Of course. That's what friends are for.

John teaches us that the strongest relationship with Christ may not necessarily be a complicated one. He teaches us that the greatest webs of loyalty are spun, not with airtight theologies or foolproof philosophies, but with friendships; stubborn, selfless, joyful friendships.

After witnessing this stubborn love, we are left with a burning desire to have one like it. We are left feeling that if we could have been in anyone's sandals that day, we would have been in young John's and would have been the one to offer a smile of loyalty to this dear Lord.

—NO WONDER THEY CALL HIM THE SAVIOR

Would you be bold tomorrow? Then be with Jesus today. Be in his Word. Be with his people. Be in his *presence*. And when *persecution* comes (and it will), be strong. Who knows, people may realize that you, like the disciples, have been with Christ.

—OUTLIVE YOUR LIFE

"If God is for us,

who can be

against us?"

—Romans 8:31 (NIV)

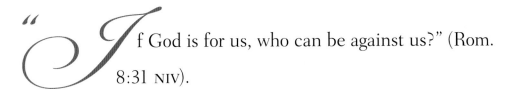

"If God is for us, who can be against us?" (Rom. 8:31 NIV).

The question is not simply, "Who can be against us?" You could answer that one. Who is against you? Disease, inflation, corruption, exhaustion. Calamities confront, and fears imprison. Were Paul's question, "Who can be against us?" we could list our foes much easier than we could fight them. But that is not the question. The question is, if *God is for us*, who can be against us?

Indulge me for a moment. Four words in this verse deserve your attention. Read slowly the phrase, "God is for us." Please pause for a minute before you continue. Read it again, aloud. (My apologies to the person next to you.) *God is for us.* Repeat the phrase four times, this time emphasizing each word. (Come on, you're not in that big of a hurry.)

God is for us.

God *is* for us.

God is *for* us.

God is for *us*.

God is for you. Your parents may have forgotten you, your teachers may have neglected you, your siblings may be ashamed of you; but within reach of your prayers is the maker of the oceans. God!

God *is* for you. Not "may be," not "has been," not "was," not "would be," but "God is!" He *is* for you. Today. At this hour. At this minute. As you read this sentence. No need to wait in line or come back tomorrow.

He is with you. He could not be closer than he is at this second. His loyalty won't increase if you are better nor lessen if you are worse. He *is* for you.

God is *for* you. Turn to the sidelines; that's God cheering your run. Look past the finish line; that's God applauding your steps. Listen for him in the bleachers, shouting your name. Too tired to continue? He'll carry you. Too discouraged to fight? He's picking you up. God is *for* you.

God is for *you*. Had he a calendar, your birthday would be circled. If he drove a car, your name would be on his bumper. If there's a tree in heaven, he's carved your name in the bark. We know he has a tattoo, and we know what it says. "I have written your name on my hand," he declares (Isa. 49:16 NCV).

"Can a mother forget the baby at her breast and have no compassion on the child she has borne?" God asks in Isaiah 49:15 (NIV). What a bizarre question. Can you mothers imagine feeding your infant and then later asking, "What was that baby's name?" No. I've seen you care for your young. You stroke the hair, you touch the face, you sing the name over and over. Can a mother forget? No way. But "even if she could forget, . . . I will not forget you," God pledges (Isa. 49:15 NCV).

God is with you. Knowing that, who is against you? Can death harm you now? Can disease rob your life? Can your purpose be taken or your value diminished? No. Though hell itself may set itself against you, no one can defeat you. You are protected. God is with you.

—IN THE GRIP OF GRACE

As I boarded a plane once, the pilot called my name. He was standing in the cockpit entrance, greeting passengers. "Well, hello, Max." I looked up. It was my friend Joe. My old friend. He is the Methuselah of the airways. He's been flying forever. He flew transports in Vietnam and has logged a bookful of hours as a commercial pilot. He's faced every flight crisis from electrical storms to empty fuel tanks. He is a good pilot.

And he is a friend, a good friend. He's not my neighbor, but if he were, our property value would increase. If I were in the hospital, he'd keep a bedside vigil. If I were on vacation, he'd keep my dog. If I offended him, he'd keep his cool until we could talk it through. He could no more tell a lie than a mosquito could sing the national anthem. He never swears, gets drunk, cheats, or swindles. He is that good.

He is good—good in skill and good in heart.

We chatted for a few minutes, and I went to my seat with a sense of assurance. *What more could I request? I thought. The pilot is experienced and proven. Even more, he is my tried-and-true friend. I am in good hands.*

The knowledge came in handy. An hour into the flight we hit a wall of winds. People gasped, dentures rattled, and the attendant told us to check our seat belts and rosary beads. I've had smoother roller coaster rides. Unlike the other passengers, however, I stayed calm. I didn't have a death wish, but I had an advantage. I knew the pilot. I knew Joe. I knew his heart and trusted his skill. *Joe can handle this*, I told myself. The storm was bad, but the pilot was good. So as much as one can relax in a squall, I did.

Friend, it's a stormy world out there. Every day brings turbulence. Moody economy. Aging bodies. Declining job market. Increasing street violence. The question during these troubling times is this: Do we have a good pilot?

The resounding response of the Bible is yes!

— BEFORE AMEN

You are
good,
LORD.

—Psalm 25:7 (NCV)

Good and *upright* is the LORD.

—Psalm 25:8 (NIV)

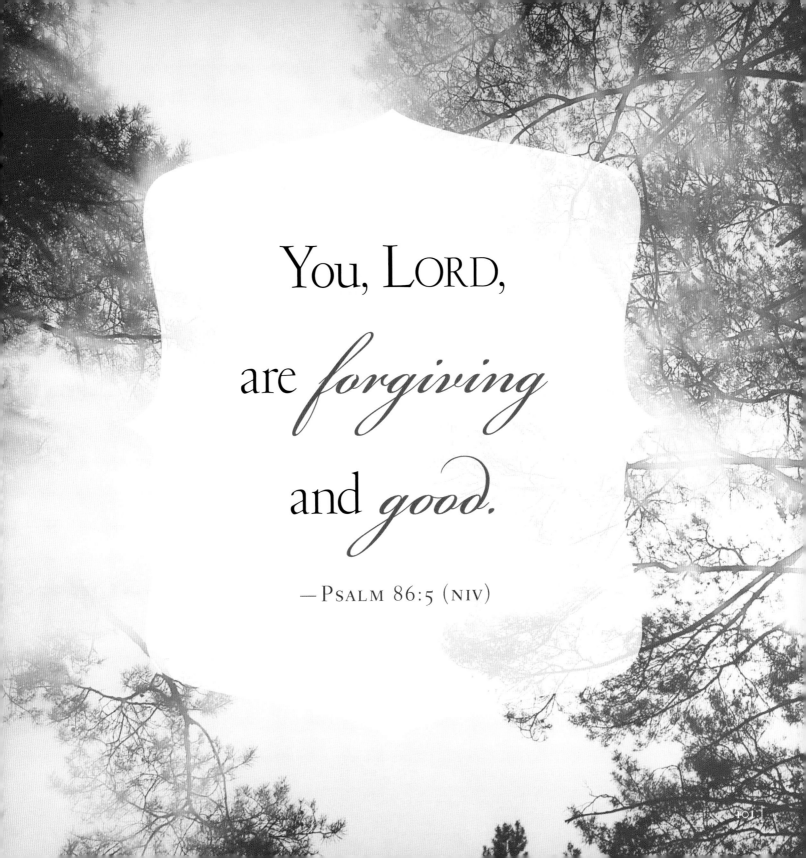

You, LORD,

are *forgiving*

and *good.*

—PSALM 86:5 (NIV)

If God were only *mighty,* we would salute him. But since he is *merciful* and mighty, we can approach him.

—BEFORE AMEN

Not to us, O LORD,

not to us, but to Your name

give *glory* because of

Your lovingkindness,

because of Your *truth.*

—PSALM 115:1 (NASB)

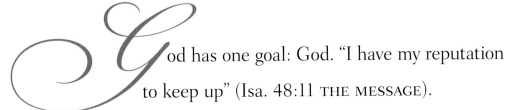

od has one goal: God. "I have my reputation to keep up" (Isa. 48:11 THE MESSAGE).

Surprised? Isn't such an attitude, dare we ask, self-centered? Don't we deem this behavior self-promotion? Why does God broadcast himself?

For the same reason the pilot of the lifeboat does. Think of it this way. You're floundering neck-deep in a dark, cold sea. Ship sinking. Life jacket deflating. Strength waning. Through the inky night comes the voice of a lifeboat pilot. But you cannot see him. What do you want the driver of the lifeboat to do?

Be quiet? Say nothing? Stealth his way through the drowning passengers? By no means! You need volume! Amp it up, buddy! In biblical jargon, you want him to show his glory. You need to hear him say, "I am here. I am strong. I have room for you. I can save you!" Drowning passengers want the pilot to reveal his preeminence.

Don't we want God to do the same? Look around. People thrash about in seas of guilt, anger, despair. Life isn't working. We are going down fast. But God can rescue us. And only one message matters. His! We need to see God's glory.

Make no mistake. God has no ego problem. *He does not reveal his glory for his good. We need to witness it for ours.* We need a strong hand to pull us into a safe boat. And, once aboard, what becomes our priority?

Simple. Promote God. We declare his preeminence. "Hey! Strong boat over here! Able pilot! He can pull you out!"

Passengers promote the pilot. "Not to us, O Lord, not to us, but to

Your name give glory because of Your lovingkindness, because of Your truth" (Ps. 115:1 NASB). If we boast at all, we "boast in the Lord" (2 Cor. 10:17 NASB).

The breath you took as you read that last sentence was given to you for one reason, that you might for another moment "reflect the Lord's glory" (2 Cor. 3:18 NIV). God awoke you and me this morning for one purpose: "Declare his glory among the nations, his marvelous deeds among all peoples" (1 Chron. 16:24 NIV).

—IT'S NOT ABOUT ME

God does not

reveal his *glory*

for his good.

We need to

witness

it for ours.